P9-BEE-822

Rye Public Library
581 Washington Road
Rye, New Hampshire 03870

Machines at Work
Tractors

by Wendy Strobel Dieker

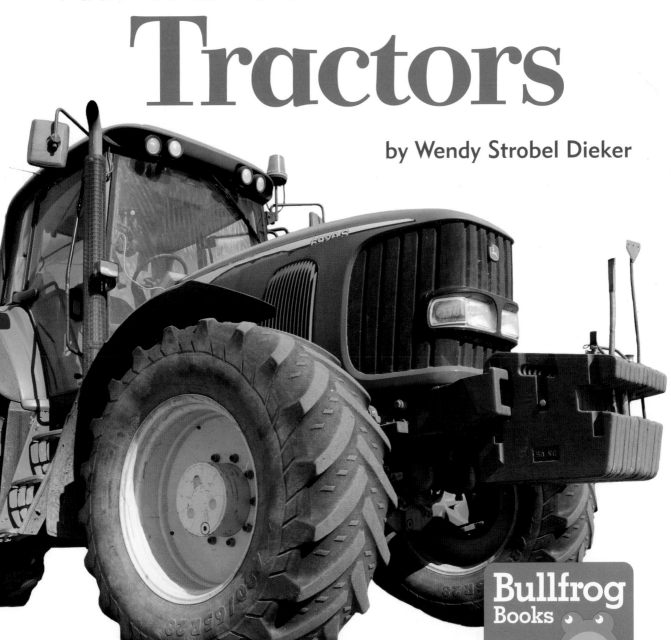

Bullfrog Books

Ideas for Parents and Teachers

Bullfrog Books give children practice reading informational text at the earliest levels. Repetition, familiar words, and photo labels support early readers.

Before Reading

- Discuss the cover photo. What does it tell them?

- Look at the picture glossary together. Read and discuss the words.

Read the Book

- "Walk" through the book and look at the photos. Let the child ask questions.

- Read the book to the child, or have him or her read independently.

After Reading

- Prompt the child to think more. Ask: Have you seen a big tractor? Where have you seen small tractors? Would you want to ride in a tractor?

Bullfrog Books are published by Jump!
5357 Penn Avenue South
Minneapolis, MN 55419
www.jumplibrary.com

Copyright © 2013 Jump! International copyright reserved in all countries. No part of this book may be reproduced in any form without written permission from the publisher.

Library of Congress Cataloging-in-Publication Data
Dieker, Wendy Strobel.
Tractors / by Wendy Strobel Dieker
  p. cm. — (Bullfrog books. Machines at work)
Audience: K to grade 3
 Summary: "This photo-illustrated book for early readers describes the parts of a tractor and the tools it pulls for different jobs on the farm. Includes picture glossary"—Provided by publisher.
 Includes bibliographical references and index.
 ISBN 978-1-62031-023-6 (hardcover : alk. paper)
1. Tractors—Juvenile literature. I. Title.
TL233.15.G57 2013
629.225'2—dc23   2012009097

Series Editor: Rebecca Glaser
Series Designer: Ellen Huber
Photo Researcher: Heather Dreisbach

Photo Credits: Dreamstime.com, 6, 14; Getty Images, 7; iStockphoto, 1, 3, 4, 20t, 22; John Deere, 11; Shutterstock, 8–9, 10, 16, 17, 20b, 23bl, 23br, 23ml, 23mr, 23tl, 24; Superstock, 5, 12–13, 14–15, 18, 21, 23tr

Printed in the United States of America at Corporate Graphics, North Mankato, Minnesota.
7-2012 • PO 1122
10 9 8 7 6 5 4 3 2 1

Table of Contents

Tractors at Work

Farmers drive tractors.

How do they work?

A tractor needs big tires.

They go over bumpy ground.

A tractor tire is taller than you!

A tractor has a big engine.

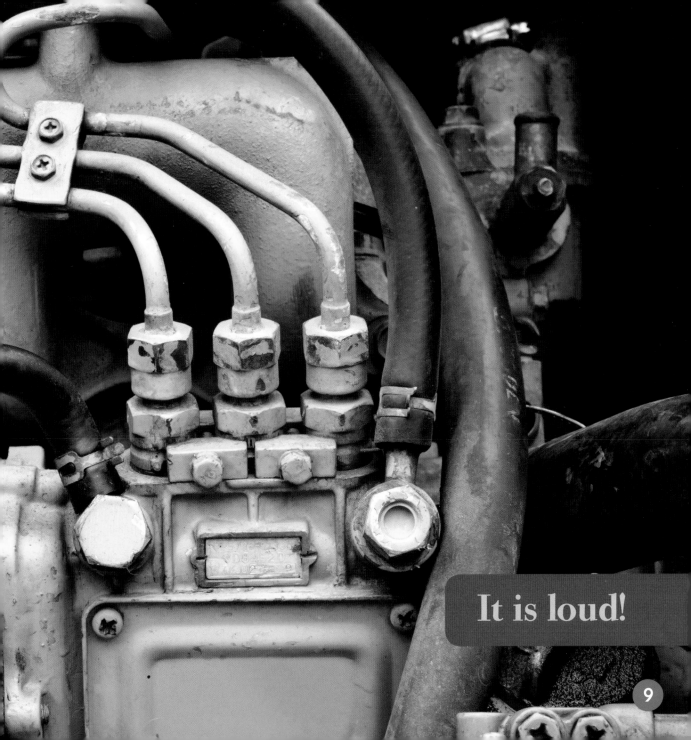

It is loud!

hitch ···▶

Tools hook onto
the hitch.

A tractor pulls
the tools.

They do field
work.

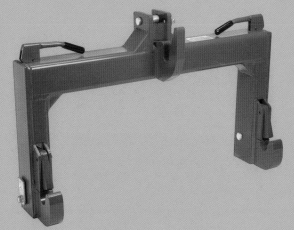

A farmer sits in the cab.
It has big windows.

She can see the field.

It is spring.

A tractor pulls a planter.

The seeds fall in a straight line.

It is summer.

A tractor pulls a sprayer.

It sprays fertilizer.
The crops grow faster.

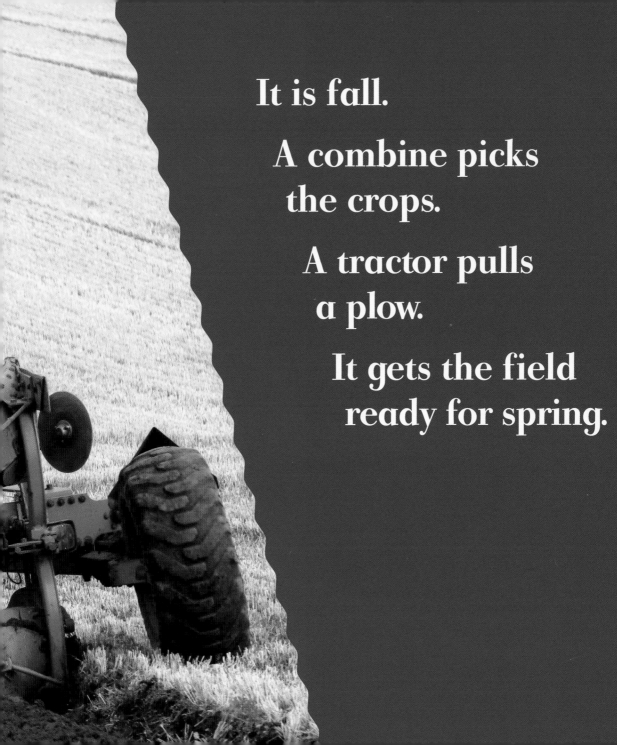

It is fall.

A combine picks
the crops.

A tractor pulls
a plow.

It gets the field
ready for spring.

Tractors do many farm jobs!

Parts of a Tractor

cab
The part of a tractor where a driver sits.

hitch
The part on the back of a tractor where tools are hooked up.

tire
The rubber part on a wheel that is filled with air.

Picture Glossary

combine
A big farm machine, larger than a tractor, that picks crops.

planter
A farm tool that drops seeds into the field and covers them with dirt.

engine
A machine that burns fuel to make a tractor move.

plow
A farm tool that turns over the dirt to get it ready for planting.

fertilizer
A spray or dry material that helps plants grow faster and healthier.

sprayer
A farm tool that sprays fertilizer or bug spray on the crops.

Index

To Learn More

Learning more is as easy as 1, 2, 3.

1) Go to www.factsurfer.com

2) Enter "tractor" into the search box.

3) Click the "Surf" button to see a list of websites.

With factsurfer.com, finding more information is just a click away.

P9-BEE-823